CHRISTIAN HEROES: THEN & NOW

LOTTIE MOON

Unit Study

Curriculum Guide

JANET & GEOFF BENGE

YWAM PUBLISHING
A Ministry Of Youth With A Mission
P.O. Box 55787, Seattle, WA 98155

YWAM Publishing is the publishing ministry of Youth With A Mission. Youth With A Mission (YWAM) is an international missionary organization of Christians from many denominations dedicated to presenting Jesus Christ to this generation. To this end, YWAM has focused its efforts in three main areas: 1) Training and equipping believers for their part in fulfilling the Great Commission (Matthew 28:19). 2) Personal evangelism. 3) Mercy ministry (medical and relief work).

For a free catalog of books and materials write or call:
YWAM Publishing
P.O. Box 55787, Seattle, WA 98155
(425) 771-1153 or (800) 922-2143
www.ywampublishing.com

Lottie Moon: A Unit Study Curriculum Guide

10 09 08 07 06 05 04 03 02 01 10 9 8 7 6 5 4 3 2 1

Published by Youth With A Mission Publishing
P.O. Box 55787
Seattle, WA 98155

ISBN 1-57658-209-4

Printed in the United States of America.

Contents

Lottie Moon

1840–1912

Introduction

Lottie Moon: A Unit Study Curriculum Guide

This unit study guide is designed to accompany the book *Lottie Moon: Giving Her All for China* from the Christian Heroes: Then & Now series by Janet and Geoff Benge. It provides the Christian school teacher and homeschooling parent with ways to use the book as a vehicle for teaching or reinforcing various curriculum areas, including

- Creative writing.
- Drama.
- Movie critiquing.
- Reading comprehension.
- Essay writing.
- History and geography concepts.

As there are more ideas than could possibly be used in one unit, it is the parent/teacher's job to sift through the ideas and select those that best fit the needs of the students.

The activities recommended in this unit study guide are

- Reflective of a wide range of learning styles.
- Designed for both group and individual study.
- Suitable for a range of grade levels and abilities.

Learning Styles

Choose those activities that are best suited to your student or students. For example, when studying the physical features of a country, a kinesthetic learner will learn best by producing a three-dimensional clay model representing the physical features of the country, whereas a visual learner will find it more meaningful to produce a poster map of the country for the classroom wall.

Group or Individual Study

While the activities contained in this unit study guide are designed to be carried out by a student working alone, instructions are also provided for adapting an activity to a group situation.

Grade Levels/Abilities

As you thumb through this unit study guide, you will note that grade levels are not assigned to particular activities, though some areas, essay topics for example, progress from the simple to the complex. This approach has been taken because students of varying grade levels can undertake most of the activities. For example, one activity calls for students to write a poem about the empty trunk that Lottie took home on her last voyage. A fourth grader doing this activity would tend to focus on the concrete objects Lottie left behind, her clothing and books for example. By contrast, a ninth grader undertaking the same assignment would be able to explore more abstract concepts such as the way in which Lottie gave up everything, not only her material goods but also her intellectual pursuits and her chance at marriage, to reach out to the Chinese people. Each student uses the same activity and instructions to create work appropriate to his or her age and cognitive ability.

In the center of this unit study guide you will find two foldout pages. These pages contain three maps and a fact sheet to be filled out by the student. The maps and fact sheet are designed to be photocopied onto individual pages so that each student can store them in his or her folder. They are for use with the social studies section of this unit study guide (chapter 6).

Before you begin teaching from this unit study guide, please read through each section. You may wish to highlight the activities that appeal to you or that you know your students would enjoy or be challenged by. Many teachers find it useful to plan the culminating event (see chapter 8) first and then select a range of learning activities that lend themselves to this event.

For the sake of brevity in the instructions that accompany each section, the word *teacher* includes the homeschooling parent, and the word *student* refers to a child either in a traditional classroom or in a homeschool environment.

1

Key Bible Verses

The authors have selected four Bible verses that can be used alongside or as part of this unit study. For your convenience, these verses have been quoted in two versions: the King James Version and the New International Version. Of course, many other appropriate Bible verses can be added to the list if more are needed. These verses can be used in a number of ways. Four ideas for using them are listed below.

Memorization. The teacher can assign one or all of the verses to be memorized during the duration of the study. A chart could be made to track which students have completed memorizing which verses.

Meaning. The verses can be used to spark conversations on the spiritual aspects of Lottie's life. This can then be translated into action by having students form groups and present one of the verses to the class in a creative manner. Students could make up a skit to illustrate the meaning of the verse or present a one-act play to show how the verse was relevant in the life of Lottie Moon.

Devotional. The teacher might also consider beginning a class or family devotional book. To do this, the teacher should familiarize the students with a variety of devotional writings and then ask them to write a devotion based upon their own understanding of one of the verses as it relates to the life of Lottie Moon. The pages could then be glued or copied into a blank book, illustrated, and signed. The various devotions could be read aloud at appropriate times, including during assemblies and family devotional times and at the culminating event.

Display. Students could also design a plaque, wall hanging, poster, or banner with one of the verses written on it. This could be hung in a prominent place while the unit study is being undertaken and used for decoration during the culminating event.

“Trust in the Lord, and do good; so shalt thou dwell in the land, and verily thou shalt be fed” (Psalm 37:3 KJV).

“Trust in the Lord and do good; dwell in the land and enjoy safe pasture” (Psalm 37:3 NIV).

“He that covereth a transgression seeketh love; but he that repeateth a matter separateth very friends” (Proverbs 17:9 KJV).

“He who covers over an offense promotes love, but whoever repeats the matter separates close friends” (Proverbs 17:9 NIV).

❝And he said unto them, Take heed, and beware of covetousness: for a man's life consisteth not in the abundance of the things which he possesseth❞ (Luke 12:15 KJV).

❝Then he said to them, "Watch out! Be on your guard against all kinds of greed; a man's life does not consist in the abundance of his possessions❞ (Luke 12:15 NIV).

❝Every man according as he purposeth in his heart, so let him give; not grudgingly, or of necessity: for God loveth a cheerful giver❞ (2 Corinthians 9:7 KJV).

❝Each man should give what he has decided in his heart to give, not reluctantly or under compulsion, for God loves a cheerful giver❞ (2 Corinthians 9:7 NIV).

2

Display Corner

Many students will enjoy collecting and displaying objects related to the places or events they are studying. It is motivational to designate a corner of the room, including a table or desk and wall space that can be used for this purpose. Keep some index cards on the table and encourage students to label their contributions, including as much information as possible about where each object came from, what it is used for, and who would use it.

Encourage students to ask their parents and friends if they have anything interesting (but not valuable) from China that they could bring to class. A visit to an Asian grocery could also yield some very interesting display items, as would a trip to the local library to find books on China and famous Chinese people and inventions. Students might also like to bring information or artifacts that relate to the life and work of Lottie Moon. Following is a list of things students (or you) might like to display. Of course, there are many more options.

- A large map of China.
- Items of Chinese clothing, including slippers, padded jackets, and woven hats.
- Chinese food and food-related objects, such as rice, spices, noodles, dried foods, bowls, tea, teapots and cups, and cookbooks.
- Examples of Chinese writing, including Bibles and tracts. These are available through the American Bible Society at (800) 32-BIBLE or online at www.americanbible.org.
- Photographs and articles about China, both in the past and in the present.
- Newspaper articles about China that highlight current events in the various regions of the country.
- Chinese stamps and coins.
- Dolls in native Chinese dress.
- Books and photographs about pre-war Virginia.
- Books and photographs about the American Civil War.
- A red paper banner with the words to a simple children's chorus written on it.
- A recipe for sugar cookies.
- A small, empty trunk.

3

Chapter Questions

There are four questions related to each chapter of *Lottie Moon: Giving Her All for China.*

1. A vocabulary question drawn from the text and referenced to a page in the book.
2. A factual question arising from the text.
3. A question to gauge the level of a student's comprehension.
4. An open-ended question seeking an opinion or interpretation.

These questions are designed for students to complete on their own. They are best answered as a student finishes reading each chapter in the book. Answers to the first three questions for each chapter are given in Appendix B. The answer to the fourth question is open ended and needs to be evaluated separately. Since question four deals with a student's interpretation or opinions, it is a good question on which to base a group discussion. Keep in mind that there is no right or wrong answer to question four, just positions a student needs to justify.

To gain maximum benefit from the questions, the students should write full-sentence answers and not just one or two words. For example, in response to the question "How many people lived in the Tengchow area?" they should write "Eighty thousand people lived in the Tengchow area," and not the lone words, "Eighty thousand."

Each vocabulary question asks the students to use the new word in a sentence. If you ask them to do this, make sure their sentences clearly demonstrate the meaning of the vocabulary word.

As a supplement to answering the questions, you may ask the students to write a short summary of each chapter or write a response to the chapter in their journals. This could involve the students writing about how they relate to Lottie Moon's actions, noting how they think they would react in a similar situation, and speculating as to what they think might happen next in the story.

Chapter One

1. What is a benefactor (page 14)? Use the word in a sentence.
2. How large was the Viewmont plantation?
3. At the time of her grandmother's death, how many children were there in Lottie Moon's family?
4. What did you learn about Lottie's character from chapter 1?

Chapter Two

1. What does scandalous mean (page 26)? Use the word in a sentence.

2. What was Lottie's father carrying on his back when he collapsed?
3. Why did Lottie decide to pull the prank that she did?
4. Do you think Lottie should have spent so much money on her education when she had no idea what she wanted to do with it?

Chapter Three

1. What is a homily (page 38)? Use the word in a sentence.
2. What did Lottie tell the class her middle initial "D" stood for?
3. Why didn't Lottie go overseas with Orie?
4. Why do you think that Lottie never considered becoming a doctor like her sister Orie?

Chapter Four

1. What does piqued mean (page 54)? Use the word in a sentence.
2. How many southern men died in the Civil War?
3. Why didn't the Southern Baptist Church send out any missionaries during the Civil War?
4. What do you think were some things southerners found difficult to forgive northerners for after the Civil War?

Chapter Five

1. What does assailing mean (page 64)? Use the word in a sentence.
2. What was the name of the secretary of the Foreign Mission Board?

3. Why was Lula Whilden allowed to become a missionary even though she was a single woman?
4. Do you think Lottie would have found a way to get to China as a missionary if her sister had not gone out before her? Why or why not?

Chapter Six

1. What does ominously mean (page 72)? Use the word in a sentence.
2. How many people lived in the Tengchow area?
3. Why did Lottie and Martha have to travel overland to Tengchow?
4. What were some of the challenges that Eddie and Lottie might face if they moved out of the Crawfords' house?

Chapter Seven

1. What are dialects (page 85)? Use the word in a sentence.
2. Approximately how many preaching trips a year did Sallie Holmes make into the country?
3. Why did Lottie have difficulty learning Mandarin even though she knew several other languages?
4. Why do you think Lottie admired Sallie Holmes so much?

Chapter Eight

1. What does obstinate mean (page 101)? Use the word in a sentence.
2. Where did Lottie and Eddie spend Christmas of 1876?

3. Why didn't Lottie and Eddie need to use the money for their house right away?
4. Why do you think Lottie was able to continue missionary work in China when her sister Edmonia suffered a breakdown?

Chapter Nine

1. What does reticence mean (page 116)? Use the word in a sentence.
2. How many girls attended Lottie's school when it first opened in 1878?
3. Why did Lottie write to the editor of the *Biblical Recorder?*
4. Do you think there was any point in educating Chinese girls during the 1870s? Why or why not?

Chapter Ten

1. What does ravages mean (page 123)? Use the word in a sentence.
2. Why did Sallie Holmes finally go back to the United States?
3. Lottie wrote, "We need to make friends before we can hope to make converts." How did Lottie set about making friends with the people of P'ingtu?
4. Lottie took Greek and Latin books with her to P'ingtu to keep her mind stimulated. Why do you think keeping her mind alert was so important to Lottie?

Chapter Eleven

1. What does recuperate mean (page 133)? Use the word in a sentence.

2. What slogan did Lottie make up to try to recruit more missionaries to North China?
3. Which two groups of people helped establish the Woman's Missionary Union?
4. Why do you think the Southern Baptists sent out more missionaries when seven of the last ten they sent either died or returned home in broken health? Explain your answer.

Chapter Twelve

1. What does inexplicably mean (page 148)? Use the word in a sentence.
2. Whom did Lottie go to Sha-ling to protect from an angry mob?
3. Why were the Christians in Sha-ling stunned when Li Show-ting decided to become a Christian?
4. What do you think enabled Lottie to carry on with her missionary work when so many others gave up?

Chapter Thirteen

1. What does exuberant mean (page 157)? Use the word in a sentence.
2. What was the name of the group Tarleton Crawford formed?
3. Lottie waited six months after her arrival in Virginia before she began speaking to churches and groups. Why was that?
4. How do you think Lottie felt when she heard the news that Tarleton Crawford and many other missionaries had left the Southern Baptist Mission? Why?

Chapter Fourteen

1. What does quaint mean (page 169)? Use the word in a sentence.
2. Which church provided most of the money to build the hospital at Hwanghsien?
3. Why did Lottie refuse to consider spending her old age in the United States?
4. What character traits would it take to remain friends with missionaries on both sides of a very nasty split?

Chapter Fifteen

1. What does antagonism mean (page 179)? Use the word in a sentence.
2. What is the color of celebration in China?
3. Why was the Foreign Mission Board constantly short of money?
4. Can you think of a better way the mission board might have raised the money it needed?

Chapter Sixteen

1. What are hallucinations (page 193)? Use the word in a sentence.
2. How long did the Manchu Dynasty rule China?
3. Why was Lottie horrified that Chinese Christians had smashed down idols in the temple?
4. Do you think Lottie was right to refuse to bear arms, even though it meant she could not protect herself? Explain your answer.

Chapter Seventeen

1. What does evoking mean (page 201)? Use the word in a sentence.
2. In what year was the annual Christmas Offering renamed in honor of Lottie Moon?
3. How did Southern Baptists try to "make amends to Lottie" after her death?
4. If Lottie were alive today, what do you think she might say to churches in the United States?

4

Student Explorations

Student explorations are a variety of activities that are appropriate to a wide range of learning styles. These activities consist of the following:

Essay Questions. These are questions that can be used as essay writing ideas. Students can either be assigned a topic or choose their own from the list. The simplest essay topics appear first, followed in order by those that are more complex.

Creative Writing. This includes writing such things as newspaper articles, poems, letters, resumés, songs, and journals.

Hands-On Projects. These are various kinds of projects, such as charts and graphs, models, comic strips, family crests, mottoes, dioramas, book covers, and mobiles.

Audio/Visual Projects. These involve such things as using a tape recorder to conduct a mock interview or to produce a radio play or commercial, or using still and video cameras to create dramatic presentations.

Arts and Crafts. These include art forms and crafts used in China.

Language Examples. Some examples of words written in the Mandarin language are given. Students can use them to make banners or place mats for the culminating event or in their hands-on projects. For example, they could use the words on the offering box activity outlined in the arts and crafts section.

[Note on group projects: All the suggestions described below are individual learning activities. However, some of the activities have bracketed paragraphs like this one after them that offer suggestions on how the activity can be adapted for class or group use.]

Essay Questions

1. Despite the fact that Lottie had a very privileged childhood, she was able to adapt to living in meager conditions in China. Using examples from the book, discuss how and why she was able to be content living in China.

2. Research the Seneca Falls Convention and the Women's Rights Movement. Explain what the women involved were fighting for, and assess how successful they were.

3. The Civil War was among the most defining events in Lottie's life. Explore ways in which Lottie's life may have been different if the Civil War had not taken place.

4. In a letter home Lottie wrote, "We need to make friends before we can hope to make converts" (page 129). Use examples from Lottie's life to illustrate how she tried to live by this advice.

5. Evaluate the following quote in terms of Lottie's life. "A pessimist sees the difficulty in every opportunity; an optimist sees the opportunity in every difficulty" (Sir Winston Churchill).

Creative Writing

1. When Lottie died, all that she possessed was an empty trunk. Write a poem about that trunk and what it says about Lottie's life.
2. Write a series of three letters in Lottie's voice that describes events in her life. For example, you might write about her father dying or about her going away to school, becoming a Christian, being a Civil War nurse, or choosing to become a missionary.
3. Write and illustrate a children's book about the life and influence of Lottie Moon.
4. Southern Baptist Churches dedicated memorials to Lottie Moon. Make a plaque with what you consider to be an appropriate inscription on it.
5. Make a brochure to help recruit potential missionaries for Lottie's "Thirty Seed-sowers for North China" campaign (see pages 139–140).

Hands-On Projects

1. Make a timeline of Lottie's life. On the timeline also record the major world events that occurred. For example, the Civil War and the major events in the woman-suffrage movement (the fight for the right to vote).
   [This can be an individual or a group effort.]

2. Make a poster that shows the contrasts between the privileged life Lottie enjoyed in her youth and her lifestyle in P'ingtu.

3. Research the growth of railroads in the United States. Make a poster map showing the main railroad routes, along with when they were completed. Indicate on the map which routes Lottie traveled and when.

4. Select or make models of five objects that represent significant events in Lottie's life. Make up a display explaining why you consider them significant. For example, you might include a branch to represent her love of climbing trees as a child, a replica of a degree certificate, a Latin or Greek book, a ticket on the *Costa Rica*, or two bowls to represent the idea that she always shared her food with others.
[Coordinate the "artifacts" and present them in a display. Have the students prepare an audio tour of the artifacts, telling how they reflect aspects of Lottie's life.]

5. Make a large red scroll and write the words of your favorite children's chorus on it. Use the scroll to teach a group of children the words to the song.

6. Lottie suggested that an offering for missionaries should be taken up at Christmas time. Brainstorm ways your family or school could raise money for a missionary. Come up with a plan, carry it out, and send a check and letter off to that missionary. You might like to consider inviting other groups to join in and making this an annual event.

7. Research how your church or denomination supports missionaries. Draw a graph to show how much money is given to various missionary causes and mark on a map the places where these supported missionaries serve.

Audio/Visual Projects

1. Research the life of Elizabeth Blackwell (America's first female doctor). Write and perform a monologue in which she explains her life, her achievements, and the obstacles she had to overcome to pursue a career in medicine. Tape-record the monologue. *[Play the monologue back to the group and have them compare and contrast Elizabeth Blackwell's struggle to the obstacles Lottie had to overcome to be a missionary.]*
2. Write a short skit about a present-day boy or girl who is trying to work out what the Lottie Moon Offering is all about. Videotape the skit and share it with your class or Sunday school.
3. Imagine you are Lottie Moon. However, instead of just sending letters back home to the United States you are able to send video conversations. Produce a video letter telling about some event that happened to you in China.

Arts and Crafts

1. Research the land and homes of the pre–Civil War plantations. Paint or draw a picture of what the Viewmont plantation might have looked like.
2. Many churches made "Lottie Moon Offering Boxes" for their congregations to take home and fill with

money. Design and produce your own Lottie Moon Offering Box.

3. Make sugar cookies using Lottie's recipe:

   2 cups of flour
   1/4 pound of butter
   1 heaped cup of sugar
   1 egg, well beaten
   1 tablespoon of milk

   Soften the butter and mix in the sugar. (This is called creaming the butter and sugar.) Stir in the remaining ingredients. Roll into balls and place on a floured cookie sheet. Bake at 450 degrees Fahrenheit for ten minutes.

Language Examples

Below are several examples of words written in the Mandarin language. Use these words to make banners, posters, and bookmarks, as well as on invitations or place mats for the culminating event.

笑口常開

Always keep smiling.

中國

China

宣教士

missionary

You can also see examples of Chinese writing online at numerous websites. To find current sites, search using the key words "Chinese calligraphy."

5

Community Links

Many communities have a rich supply of people and places to which students can be exposed to help them learn about and appreciate other cultures. It is well worth the effort to find out what your community has to offer with regard to the unit you are studying. For this unit, for example, you may be able to visit a Chinese Christian church and interview some of its members, or you could possibly find a Chinese restaurant near you that you could tour.

While it would be wonderful if you could take a field trip to visit some of these people and places, if you can't, it is often possible to have visitors come to the classroom. Whether you decide to take a field trip or invite a guest to your classroom, such activities need to be flanked by sound educational choices. Otherwise much of the educational value of the event will not be realized. The following three steps will help students derive the greatest educational value from a field trip or classroom visit.

Step One: Preparation

Students should always research the topic before they begin a classroom interview or field trip. In doing so they will be ready to ask intelligent questions based upon a sound knowledge of their topic. For example, if a class is going to a museum exhibit featuring Civil War artifacts, make sure they have already read some additional information about the Civil War.

As the teacher, you need to give the students a clear idea as to why they are going on the field trip and what they are expected to produce with their findings. For example, you might say to them, "We are going to visit an exhibit on the Civil War. Each group is going to be in charge of one area of research (e.g., home life, slavery, medicine, soldiers, politics, etc.). When we get back, I expect each group to produce a poster representing its area of research, including sketches of at least five related objects you saw at the exhibit."

Students should be encouraged to compile lists of questions they want answers to, based upon what they have already learned. They should carry a clipboard with them to write down answers, draw sketches, and note observations. (For less motivated students, a simple worksheet of activities to be completed on the field trip itself can be a good idea.) Such activities reinforce the idea that the field trip is a serious educational event and that the student is there to gather information, not just to be a sightseer.

Step Two: The Event

During the field trip or classroom visit, make sure that the students remain on task. Insist that they be respectful of property and other people at all times. Make sure that you have a spokesperson designated to thank whomever you talk to as well as the parents who help with the event.

Step Three: Processing and Reflection

Students should be given time to process the information they have gathered from their field trip or classroom visit and reflect on it, both individually and as a class. This can take many forms, including making flow charts or diagrams of what they learned, editing interviews for articles or audiovisual presentations, writing reports, and making booklets. Something as simple as a class book called *Did You Know?* in which each student writes down one fact he or she learned from the field trip can serve as an effective reflection tool.

Suggested Community Links

Chinese Church. Locate a Chinese church in your area. Call the pastor and ask permission to take your class for a visit. (Attending a Sunday service would be ideal here if you could arrange it with the students' families.) Be sure to check to see whether the church has a dress code or any special customs the students (and you) should be aware of. If attending a Sunday service is not possible, ask if you can visit the pastor at church or if the pastor can come to school to speak to your class.

Chinese People. People are some of the best resources of all. Perhaps a Chinese family lives in your neighborhood. You could invite a member of the family to address the class so that students can learn about the family's history. How long has the family been in the United States? What part of China is the family from? What made their family emigrate? What Chinese customs does the family still practice in America?

Chinese Restaurant. Many communities have at least one Chinese restaurant. Visit the restaurant at a nonbusy time (between two and three in the afternoon is normally a good time) and ask the owner if he or she would give your class a demonstration of how a few Chinese foods are cooked and the opportunity to taste some of them. For a small fee, perhaps your class could have a cooking lesson or a sample meal at a time when the restaurant is not busy.

Retired Missionaries. Ask around to see if you can find a retired missionary who has worked in China or Taiwan. If so, invite him or her to speak to your class. Ask the person to bring any artifacts he or she has and dress in national costume if possible. This will make the visit more memorable for the students.

Museum. Do you have a museum nearby that has an exhibit on the Civil War? If so, take the class to visit the museum and have the students identify some of the things Lottie would have been familiar with.

6

Social Studies

The social studies section is divided into five categories, each with suggestions on how to use the material given. The categories are briefly described below.

Places. This section covers significant places related to the story and named in the text of the book *Lottie Moon: Giving Her All for China.*

Journey. This category covers Lottie Moon's journey from San Francisco to Tengchow.

Terms/Vocabulary. This section gives ideas for studying some of the terms used in the book.

Geographical Characteristics. This section contains suggestions for mapping some of the physical characteristics of China.

Conceptual Questions. This section provides the teacher with conceptual social studies questions related to the book.

Places

These places are categorized by country, with the page number where they are first referred to in the book given in parentheses. Students can undertake a range of activities with these place names. They can:

- Locate and mark the places on the relevant country map. (Maps for this purpose are located in the foldout map section in the center of this guide.) Students may need to consult several maps (including historical maps) to find the locations of some of the lesser-known places mentioned.
- Note other points, such as their absolute location (latitude and longitude), and then observe how this location compares to other locations mentioned in the book. For example, calculate which location is closer to the equator or the North Pole.
- Calculate the relative locations of various places mentioned in the book. For example, how far is it from Virginia to Shanghai or from Shanghai to Tengchow?
- Construct a key to show population density in China.
- Explore how some of the place names have changed since the time of the story and give reasons for such changes.
- Pinpoint the places on a large wall map in the classroom. Students can then use index cards to write explanations as to why the places are mentioned in the story. Each card could be pinned to the wall with a length of yarn connecting it to the appropriate place on the map.

Places in the United States

Scottsville, Virginia (11)
New Orleans, Louisiana (13)
Charlottesville, Virginia (20)
Leavenworth, Kansas (29)
Fort Sumter (41)
Richmond, Virginia (46)
Appomattox, Virginia (46)
Danville, Kentucky (53)
Cartersville, Georgia (57)
San Francisco, California (66)
Crewe, Virginia (169)

Places in China

Shanghai (72)
Chefoo (77)
Tengchow (77)
Hwanghsien (124)
P'ingtu (124)
Sha-ling (139)
Laichow (159)

Other Places

Jerusalem (19)
Yokohama, Japan (71)
Kobe, Japan (72)
Nagasaki, Japan (72)
Fukuoka, Japan (166)

Journey

Using Lottie Moon's journey from San Francisco to Tengchow, China, students can

- Map the journey on the relevant map.
- Where possible, add details to the map from the story, such as how long the journey took, when Lottie started and finished her journey, and the kinds of transportation she used along the way.
- Compare the journey Lottie took to taking the same journey today. Students could research how they might reach those destinations today, how long it would take to get there, and how much it would cost.

Places Lottie Moon traveled through or near on her journey

San Francisco (71)
Yokohama, Japan (72)
Kobe, Japan (72)
Nagasaki, Japan (72)
Shanghai, China (72)
Chefoo, China (77)
Tengchow, China (77)

Terms/Vocabulary

Following is a list of terms used in the book. The page number where the term is first used is given in parentheses. The list covers a range of terms from the simple to the advanced. Students can use this list to

- Define and memorize the terms. You may find it helpful to asterisk or highlight in some way those terms you think would be appropriate for your students. If they know the meaning of all but five of the terms, have them learn only those five. Conversely, if they are unfamiliar with most of the terms, choose a realistic number for each student to explore and learn.
- Produce an individual or class reference book of terms. Assign each student a set number of terms to write a definition for or draw a sketch of. From this research, a book of definitions can be made, with one page allotted for each definition. This book could be added to throughout the year. (Students may need a dictionary to help them here.)
- Play reinforcement games such as *Go Fish*. To do this, draw some of the sketched definitions from the list compiled in the point above onto index cards and have the students take turns pairing them with written definitions.

Terms/vocabulary

plantations (13)
foothills (16)
port (18)
gold rush (28)
harbor (41)
crops (44)
transcontinental (66)
state line (67)
prairies (68)
bay (71)
coastline (71)
hurricane (72)
treaty port (76)
peninsula (77)
village (89)
famine (107)
province (123)
temperate coastal climate (132)

Geographical Characteristics

Be aware that some maps of China use different names for physical features and locations. Have students use an atlas to locate the following and then mark them on the blank map of China from the fold-out map section in the center of this book:

- China's three major rivers, their sources, and their courses: the Yangtze River, the Huang Ho or Yellow River, and the Si Kiang or West River.
- The four major regions: North, Central, South China, and the Western Lands, including Tibet and the great desert basin.
- China's major mountain ranges: the Himalayas, the Pamirs, and the Tien Shan. Label the highest mountain in each range, giving its height.
- The following important cities: Sian, Lanchow, Beijing (Peking), Canton, Shanghai, Chungking, Nanking, Tientsin, Dairen, and Wuhan. Note the population of each city.
- The location of the Gobi Desert.

- The latitude and longitude lines that bisect China.
- The seas and oceans that border China: East China Sea, Yellow Sea, South China Sea, and the Pacific Ocean.
- The fourteen countries that share borders with China.
- The Great Wall of China.

Conceptual Questions

The following questions are ordered from the simple to the complex. Using these questions, you could ask students to

- Write one or more paragraphs to answer each question.
- Present an oral report to the class on one of the questions.
- Discuss the answer(s) to a question or questions in a group context.

Questions to ponder

1. How large is China compared to the United States?
2. What is the population of China compared to the population of the United States?
3. Research the life of Sun Yat-sen. What was the vision he had for China's future?
4. Lottie Moon entered China at a time when there were many treaty ports. What was a treaty port? How many were there, and who did they belong to?
5. Choose a country that had a "concession" in Shanghai. What is the nature of the relationship between that country and China today?

— 7 —

Related Themes to Explore

Any unit study has natural links to many other topics that can also be explored. While it is impossible to pursue all such links in this context, the spoke diagram on the next page shows some related topics that students might find interesting to study alongside Lottie Moon.

There are two ways you might like to integrate some of these links into your classroom. Some teachers and parents have the flexibility to be able to choose the topics their students study and even to alter their selections partway through the year. If you are able to do this, use the theme wheel to help identify other topics you might like to follow up this unit with. For example, after studying Lottie Moon your class might become interested in the medical knowledge and practice at the time of the Civil War. In that case you might embark on a unit on the history of modern medicine.

Other teachers and parents are locked in to a less flexible curriculum. If this is your situation, you may still have the ability to change the order in which topics are taught. Look through the topics listed to see whether any coincide with topics you have already scheduled for later in the year. Consider the possibility of scheduling the teaching of these topics closer to this unit so that cross-curriculum learning can take place.

LOTTIE MOON

History

- Pre–Civil War Virginia
- The Civil War
- Reconstruction in the South
- Civil War–era medicine
- The first female doctors in the United States
- The woman-suffrage movement in the United States
- Railway growth in the United States
- The Manchu Dynasty of China
- The last emperor of China
- Sun Yat-sen and the 1912 revolution

Missions

- The Church in China today
- "Tentmaking" missionary opportunities in China
- The role of single, female missionaries in the Baptist church today
- How missionaries raise support in your church or denomination

Life Skills

- Making sugar cookies

Current Events

- China and its role in world events
- Life in China today

8

Culminating Event

As adults, we like to have a reason to learn something. We learn a new computer program so that we can balance our checking account, a song so that we can sing it at a wedding, or the rudiments of another language so that we are able to find our way around in a foreign country. Students have the same need for purpose in their learning. It is valid but not very motivational to tell a student that he or she needs to gather and learn information to pass a test or move up a grade. It is much more motivational for a student when he or she has some other, more meaningful goal in mind. This goal can be a specific forum through which each student can express his or her newly acquired knowledge. We believe that part of the role of the teacher is to provide such a forum, which we call the culminating event.

As the name implies, the culminating event marks the end of the unit study and gives a sense of closure to the topic. It also serves to put what students have learned into a larger context that can then be shared with others.

The culminating event can be as simple as inviting the class next door (or the homeschooled children down the street) to come and hear poems and stories and view the written work that students have completed. Conversely, it could be as involved as hosting a parent/neighborhood dinner featuring Chinese food, songs, games, plays, and presentations on the life and achievements of Lottie Moon and the places where she served.

No matter how simple or elaborate the culminating event is, make sure you have the broad outline of it in mind before planning the other activities for your unit study, as the two are integrally linked.

Idea Sparks

Food. Prepare and serve Chinese food. Fruits and vegetables grown and eaten around the Shantung and Hopei regions include pears, peaches, apples, grapes, melons, peanuts, leeks, and onions. Meats include roast chicken, roast pork, prawns, and freshwater crab. Steamed bread, millet, and noodles are more commonly served than rice.

A typical celebration meal from this region might include steamed bread, steamed vegetables, including leeks, onions, and garlic, and boiled, roasted, or barbecued chicken or pork. The meat, which is cut into chunks, would be accompanied by bowls of dipping sauces. Some common sauces are chili-soy sauce, garlic-vinegar mix, plum sauce, and sweetened soy jam. For dessert, make Lottie's sugar cookies.

Provide chopsticks and serve Chinese tea in bowls. Seat the boys and girls separately. Eat off a low table or off a rug spread on the floor. Decorate with red paper lanterns. (Red is the color of celebration in China.)

Music. Play traditional Chinese music in the background to set the mood. (Many libraries stock ethnic music selections.)

Oral Presentations. Present poems, essays, reports, speeches, reviews, and devotions that students have written during the course of the unit study.

Display. Display other work, including artwork, map work, models, newspapers, and video interviews.

Clothing. Younger students might enjoy dressing up in Chinese dress for this event.

Cultural Activities. Play traditional Chinese children's games.

Appendix A

Books and Resources

This appendix is divided into six sections: (1) other biographies of Lottie Moon, (2) related books, (3) other books in the Christian Heroes: Then & Now series set in China, (4) related documentaries and movies, (5) related articles from *National Geographic*, and (6) Internet sites.

Many books about Lottie Moon are written at a higher reading level than the books in the Christian Heroes: Then & Now series and would be interesting for a teacher to read for his or her own information and as background for the unit. Keep in mind that children learn best by example, so consider choosing one good adult book to read and enrich your own understanding of the topic. Resources for younger children are also included, and if they can be found, they can make it easy for younger family members or less able readers to participate in the unit study at their own level.

Some of the books listed here are more difficult to get copies of than others. If they are not available at your local Christian bookstore, many of the titles can be located in secondhand bookstores (try using the Internet to locate them). Most titles are also available through the national interlibrary loan service.

Other Biographies of Lottie Moon

All the biographies listed on the bibliography page of *Lottie Moon: Giving Her All for China,* as well as others that may be of interest, are listed here. Each listing has basic information on how to locate the book, including its ISBN number. The approximate age level of the intended reader is also given, along with the number of pages in each book and some comments to help you decide whether you might want to include this book in your unit study.

TITLE: *The New Lottie Moon Story*
Author: Catherine B. Allen
Publisher: Woman's Missionary Union, 1997
ISBN: 1563092255
Age Level: Adult, 320 pages

Synopsis: This book covers every aspect of Lottie Moon's story in detail, from her family lineage to her life in China to the Lottie Moon offering established after her death. The book contains photographs, maps, and letters written by Lottie. It also has a seven-page index and extensive footnoting.

Comments: This is the definitive work on Lottie Moon. Catherine Allen served on the national staff of the Woman's Missionary Union of the Southern Baptist Convention for twenty-six years, and for much of that time she researched the details of Lottie's life and the impact she has had on present-day mission policies and practices. This book is well worth purchasing as a reference tool or for interested adults to read. (It explains the Tarleton Crawford split in great detail, and it also addresses the supposed romance between Lottie and a Professor Toy.)

TITLE:	*A Journey of Faith and Sacrifice: Retracing the Steps of Lottie Moon*
Author:	Jerry Rankin
Publisher:	Woman's Missionary Union, Birmingham, Alabama, 1996
ISBN:	1563091887
Age Level:	Adult, 110 pages

Synopsis: Jerry Rankin and photographer Don Rutledge retrace the steps of Lottie Moon. They begin with what is now left of the Viewmont plantation and continue through her school days, her time in Georgia, and on to her life in China. Throughout the book Rankin alternates between historic references to Lottie Moon and contemporary Christian life in the areas where she was a missionary pioneer.

Comments: This coffee-table book has extensive photographs of what can be found of Lottie's life today. These photos include the grounds of what was Viewmont, grandchildren of some of Lottie's converts, the house at Little Crossroads, and the remains of the hospital that Lottie raised money for. This book will help students to visualize Lottie's life.

TITLE:	*Lady of Courage: The Story of Lottie Moon*
Author:	Ann Kilner Hughes
Publisher:	Woman's Missionary Union, SBC, 1987
ISBN:	1563091593
Age Level:	8–12 years old, 63 pages

Synopsis: Hughes covers Lottie's entire life from her carefree childhood to her death and discusses the impact her life has had on Southern Baptist women and missions.

Comments: The book has lots of pencil sketches and an easy layout for younger children to read for themselves. It tells the story of Lottie's life in a simple way and would be suitable to read aloud to attentive six- or seven-year-olds.

TITLE: *Lottie Moon: A Biographical Sketch*
Author: Catherine B. Allen
Publisher: Woman's Missionary Union, SBC, undated
ISBN: 1563093847
Age Level: Adult, 6 pages

Synopsis: This booklet provides a brief sketch of Lottie's life. It is written to an adult audience.

Comments: This booklet can be purchased inexpensively from the Southern Baptist Union. While it is not written for children, it might be useful to give to parents or other interested adults in order to fill them in on Lottie's life.

TITLE: *Her Own Way: The Story of Lottie Moon*
Author: Helen A. Monsell
Publisher: Broadman Press, 1958
ISBN: 0805443193
Age Level: 8–12 years old, 188 pages

Synopsis: This is Lottie's story told for children up to about the age of twelve. The events of her life have been simplified to make them easily understandable, and there are few historical details such as dates and place names. Monsell does not cover controversial areas of Lottie's career, including the many struggles she had with other Baptist missionaries in China.

Comments: This book was obviously written to give a younger child a feeling for the adventurous and unselfish life that Lottie lived. It has black-and-white pen sketches throughout that help the reader to visualize what is happening in the story. The language is rather dated.

TITLE: *Lottie Moon*
Author: Una Roberts Lawrence
Publisher: Sunday School Board of the Southern Baptist Convention,1927
ISBN: N/A
Age Level: Adult, 317 pages

Synopsis: This book starts out by detailing the lives of Lottie's ancestors as far back as 1672. Una Roberts Lawrence began her research in 1923 and was able to interview many people who knew Lottie well, including some of her sister Orie's sons and missionaries who had worked with Lottie in her later years. Throughout the book the author seeks to give context to Lottie's life by giving the reader details on the Civil War and life in China.

Comments: This book takes some wading through, as the language is stilted and quaint. However, it is well worth reading, since it was the first and is a substantial book on Lottie Moon. Lawrence uses many quotes from Lottie's letters to bring her story alive. There are several interesting photos in the book, mainly of places and buildings Lottie would have been familiar with.

Related Books

This section lists two books that fit around the life story of Lottie Moon. ISBN number, age level, and relevant comments are included for both books.

Of course, there are many other books that relate in some way to this topic. You may want to record inside the back cover of this unit study guide the titles of other books you find particularly helpful.

TITLE: *Whole Gospel, Whole World: The Foreign Mission Board of the Southern Baptist Convention 1845–1995*
Author: William R. Estep
Publisher: Broadman & Holman, 1994
ISBN: 0805410414
Age Level: Adult, 456 pages

Synopsis: This weighty tome represents 150 years of the Baptist Foreign Mission Board (Southern Convention). The author actually begins back in 1792 with the first Baptist missionary, William Carey (an Englishman). From there he reviews the lives of Adoniram and Ann Judson, the first two American Baptist missionaries. In chapter 3 he comes to the founding of the Southern Baptist Union, and the beginnings of its own mission program. Lottie Moon and most of her contemporaries—the Yateses, the Crawfords, the Pruitts, Henry Tupper, and Annie Armstrong—are all thoroughly covered. The book also has photographs of many people, important documents, and places that would be of interest to a wider audience. (There is, for example, a photo of Pastor Li baptizing a new convert in P'ingtu and a photo of the dedication of the Hwanghsien Baptist Church.) It also has timelines throughout, which anchor the missionaries and their work to other world events.

Comments: This book is for the serious student of Baptist missionary history. It is well researched and extensively documented and indexed. I would suggest you purchase this book if you have older students who wish to do independent research on the history of Baptist missions.

TITLE: *Our Ordered Lives Confess, Three Nineteenth-Century Missionaries in East Shantung*
Author: Irwin T. Hyatt, Jr.
Publisher: Harvard University Press, 1976
ISBN: 0674647351
Age Level: Adult, 320 pages

Synopsis: This book covers the lives of three missionaries who made their homes in East Shantung province between 1852 to 1912. These missionaries are T. P. Crawford, who served with Lottie, Lottie Moon herself, and Calvin Mateer, a Presbyterian missionary. It has eighty pages of footnotes, glossary, and indexing.

Comments: The writer is an associate professor of history at Emory University, and not surprisingly this is a scholarly book commissioned by the Harvard Studies in American-East Asian Relations. It gives an often less-than-flattering view of the missionaries, especially T. P. Crawford and the rifts he appeared to create wherever he went. Lottie Moon is presented in the most positive light, though not in terms of a religious calling. This is an interesting book for a person who wants to know more about missionary politics in East Shantung and how local Chinese people perceived the missionaries.

Other Christian Heroes: Then & Now Books Set in China

TITLE: *Hudson Taylor: Deep in the Heart of China*
Authors: Janet and Geoff Benge
Publisher: YWAM Publishing, 1998
ISBN: 1576580164
Age Level: 10 years and up, 208 pages

Comments: Hudson Taylor (1832–1905) was one of the first missionaries to China. He persevered through personal trials, including the death of his wife and three of their children. Eventually he founded the China Inland Mission.

TITLE: *Gladys Aylward: The Adventure of a Lifetime*
Authors: Janet and Geoff Benge
Publisher: YWAM Publishing, 1998
ISBN: 1576580199
Age Level: 10 years and up, 208 pages

Comments: Gladys Aylward (1902–1970) overcame a poor childhood and meager education to become the first foreigner ever to be granted citizenship by the Chinese government. Her life is filled with almost unbelievable adventures, such as mediating between rioters in a Chinese prison, befriending and converting a high-ranking mandarin, and leading nearly one hundred children to safety over rugged, enemy-filled mountains during the Sino-Japanese war.

TITLE: *Eric Liddell: Something Greater Than Gold*
Authors: Janet and Geoff Benge
Publisher: YWAM Publishing, 1999
ISBN: 1576581373
Age Level: 10 years and up, 208 pages

Comments: Eric Liddell (1902–1945) is perhaps best remembered as the 400-meter Gold Medal–winning runner at the 1924 Olympic Games. The film *Chariots of Fire* depicts the events leading up to this achievement. After the Olympics, Eric followed in his father's footsteps and became a pastor and a missionary to China. He served in China until he was placed in a Japanese internment camp, where he died.

TITLE: *Jonathan Goforth: An Open Door in China*
Authors: Janet and Geoff Benge

Publisher: YWAM Publishing, 2001
ISBN: 1576581748
Age Level: 10 years and up, 208 pages

Comments: Jonathan Goforth (1859–1935) and his wife, Rosalind, set out for China from their home in Canada. They equipped their new home with "Western conveniences" and then opened it up for tours. Over a thousand Chinese people a day toured, and many stayed to hear him preach afterward. Jonathan soon gained the reputation as China's greatest evangelist, addressing crowds of up to twenty-five thousand at a time.

Related Documentaries and Movies

Listed in this section are documentaries and movies about events in Lottie Moon's life. Where applicable, the rating for each movie is included, but as with all unfamiliar material, it is prudent to preview the film before showing it to the class.

Documentaries and movies are particularly useful in showing the visual details of another place and time period. As students watch, encourage them to study the clothing, weather, crops, terrain, and other geographical features shown in the movie.

TITLE: *Remembered Forever: The Lottie Moon Story in Sign and Voice*
Director: Judith Bishop
Type: One-Woman Play
Length: 36 minutes
Rated: N/A

Comments: This is a video of a one-woman play. It is done completely in sign language, although there is a voice-over commentary. While this production would be unlikely to hold most children's attention, a child who knew sign language would probably enjoy watching it.

TITLE: *A Journey of Faith and Sacrifice*
Director: David Walker
Type: Documentary
Length: 32 minutes
Rated: N/A

Comments: This is the companion movie to the book of the same name. Dr. Jerry Rankin, president of the International Mission Board and a former missionary to Indonesia, takes a look at Lottie's life in China and intersperses it with insights from his own missionary experience. There are shots of the Viewmont land, as well as some of the homes Lottie lived in as a missionary. There is very little on Lottie's early life. This video is obviously directed at Baptist congregations to inform and inspire them into missionary support today. It is not particularly lively, and occasionally becomes "preachy." However, it would be an interesting addition to a study on Lottie Moon, especially the scenes in China and the visits to some of the churches she founded.

TITLE: *Virginia Plantations*
(The Atlas Video Library)
Director: N/A
Type: Documentary
Length: 30 minutes
Rated: N/A

Comments: This is a short documentary showcasing three prominent Virginia plantations: Mount Vernon, Shirley, and Monticello. Monticello was the plantation near the Moons' plantation of Viewmont. Although the video is not detailed, it does leave a visual impression of plantation life and the countryside around where Lottie grew up.

TITLE: *The Civil War*
Director: Ken Burns
Type: Documentary
Length: 660 minutes
Rated: N/A

Comments: This nine-part documentary takes a thorough and attention-keeping look at the events leading up to and during the Civil War. Episodes 1 and 9 are particularly interesting in relation to Lottie Moon, as they contrast southern society before and after the Civil War.

TITLE: *Gone With the Wind*
Director: Victor Fleming
Type: Movie Drama
Length: 3 hours, 55 minutes
Rated: G

Comments: This classic story of Scarlett O'Hara and her family's plantation in Georgia, Tara, begins with the start of the Civil War and follows a southern family's downturn in fortunes as the war continues. This movie covers the same period as Lottie's years growing up at Viewmont, and it is interesting to use the social context it portrays to see just how radical Lottie was in her views about a woman's role in education and missions.

Related *National Geographic* Articles

Many magazines contain articles related to this unit study. We have chosen to reference *National Geographic* because it can provide contemporaneous commentary on many events, since it dates back to the 1880s, and because it is widely available in libraries and schools throughout the country.

These articles and their accompanying photographs represent just some of those available that bear on aspects of Lottie Moon's life. They can be used in a variety of ways to support and reinforce this unit study. For example, you could have students read the article "Present Conditions in China" (December 1906) and compare that author's observations about living in China to Lottie's experience. Likewise, students could write poems or letters home from the "battlefield" based on the images in "Witness to a War: British Correspondent Frank Vizetelly" (April 1961).

Articles about Virginia and the Civil War

TITLE: Witness to a War: British Correspondent Frank Vizetelly
Issue Date: April 1961, pages 453–491

Description: This article retraces the steps of a Civil War correspondent, Frank Vizetelly. There are many excerpts from his writings that would help a student to visualize the events that took place. The article is illustrated with detailed woodcuts and interesting photographs alongside images of the same place today.

TITLE: Appomattox—Where Grant and Lee Made Peace with Honor a Century Ago
Issue Date: April 1965, pages 435–469

Description: This is a great article on the last days of the Civil War. It includes helpful maps and photographs showing houses, clothing, and weapons of the era. The author is General Ulysses S. Grant's grandson.

TITLE: The Virginians
Issue Date: November 1974, pages 588–617

Description: A good general introduction to the state of Virginia up until 1974, including photographs and historic references from the Civil War.

TITLE: Mr. Jefferson's Monticello
Issue Date: September 1966, pages 426–444

Description: This article gives a wonderful history of Monticello, Thomas Jefferson's estate. Monticello is very close to what used to be Viewmont, and Lottie's relatives owned Monticello during her early years. This article will help a student to catch a glimpse of the privileged lifestyle Lottie Moon was born into, as well as the lovely landscape of Albemarle County.

Articles about China

TITLE: The Chinese Boxers
Issue Date: July 1900, pages 281–287

Description: An article about the rising Boxer movement from a Western viewpoint. It discusses the killing of missionaries and the political context in which it occurred.

TITLE: Present Conditions in China
Issue Date: December 1906, pages 651–672

Description: This is an excellent article talking about the changes in China, including the abolition of the civil exams, which is mentioned in the Lottie Moon book. It also tells about the role of women in society, the government, and the growth of national railroads, which have a unifying effect on the country.

TITLE: Curious and Characteristic Customs of China
Issue Date: September 1910, pages 791–806

Description: A contemporary account and description of many customs that westerners found strange. This would help the reader understand what different worlds China and the United States were at the beginning of the twentieth century, and how much Lottie Moon had to adjust her way of life.

TITLE: Present Conditions in China
Issue Date: December 1911, pages 1120–1138

Description: This article gives a good explanation of how China's civil strife and anti-foreign sentiments laid the groundwork for a revolution. Great photographs of the era, though the text is not suitable for younger readers.

TITLE: Shantung—China's Holy Land
Issue Date: September 1919, pages 231–252

Description: This article has lots of good photographs and text about life in early twentieth-century Shantung Province. It covers such things as travel, food, and religious practices.

Internet Sites

The websites mentioned may well have been updated since this guide was published, and as a result they may contain information not reviewed here. Because of this, it is vital that you check them out before allowing your students to view them.

www.cvillefbc.org/heritage.html

This website contains a brief history of the Charlottesville Baptist Church, where Lottie Moon was converted. It makes reference to her contribution to Baptist life.

www.Christianitytoday.com/ch/52H/52H034.html

This site contains an article titled "Gritty Pioneers: Six Missionaries Whose Tenacity Changed China" by Kevin Miller (originally published in *Christian History,* Fall 1996). The six missionaries are: Robert Morrison, Karl Gutzlaff, Jonathan Goforth, Lottie Moon, and John and Betty Stam. Each story is about one page, and it is written in an interesting manner.

www.imb.org

This is the website for the International Mission Board of the Southern Baptist church. It contains lots of interesting information about the work of Baptist missionaries today, and many links, especially those related to the IME (International Missions Emphasis), provide a variety of information about the Lottie Moon Christmas Offering.

www.wmu.com

This is the website for the Woman's Missionary Union, the organization that established the Lottie Moon Christmas Offering. The formation of the WMU was inspired by Lottie's influence. Learn about the current-day WMU or click on Resources, then on Library Services, for information about Lottie Moon and the missions offering.

www.skyport.com/riversidebaptist/vmissionary.html

This is a great site about the impact of the Lottie Moon offering today, showing how many missionaries the offering supports. You can read e-mails from missionaries on the field and even ask them questions yourself via e-mail. This site was specifically designed with students and families in mind.

www.dwmweb.com/web/missions/lmco.html

Another great website, with testimonies from Southern Baptist missionaries about the importance of the Lottie Moon Offering.

Appendix B

Answers to Chapter Questions

Chapter One

1. A benefactor is someone who gives money or property to a specific cause or institution.
2. The Viewmont plantation covered fifteen hundred acres.
3. There were five children in Lottie's family at the time of her grandmother's death.

Chapter Two

1. Scandalous means disgraceful or shocking.
2. Lottie's father was carrying a wooden chest containing gold coins.
3. Lottie decided to use the school bell in her prank because the bell helped students keep to the schedule, and Lottie hated the schedule.

Chapter Three

1. A homily is a religious or moral speech or sermon.
2. Lottie told the class the "D" stood for Devil.
3. Lottie did not go overseas with her sister because she wanted to continue her education.

Chapter Four

1. Piqued means to have stirred or stimulated.
2. Over 135,000 southern men died in the Civil War.
3. The Southern Baptists did not send out any more missionaries because they could not afford to.

Chapter Five

1. Assailing means persistently harassing or attacking.
2. The secretary of the Foreign Mission Board was named the Reverend Henry Tupper.
3. Lula was allowed to become a missionary because she would be living with her sister and brother-in-law.

Chapter Six

1. Ominously means in a threatening manner.
2. Eighty thousand people lived in the Tengchow area.
3. Lottie and Martha traveled overland to Tengchow because the harbor was silted up and large ships could not enter it.

Chapter Seven

1. Dialects are regional or social varieties of a language that differ in grammar and vocabulary.

2. Sallie made about fifty preaching tours into the country each year.
3. Lottie had difficulty learning Mandarin because it was a tonal language, and not based on Latin, as were the other languages Lottie knew.

Chapter Eight

1. Obstinate means stubborn.
2. Lottie and Eddie spent Christmas of 1876 at Viewmont.
3. Lottie and Eddie did not need to use the money for a house right away because they moved into the Hartwells' house when the Hartwells went to the United States.

Chapter Nine

1. Reticence means reluctance or unwillingness to speak freely.
2. Five girls attended Lottie's school when it first opened in 1878.
3. Lottie wrote the letter to the *Biblical Recorder* because she was frustrated that American Christians were not aware of the hardships of foreign missionary work.

Chapter Ten

1. Ravages are the damage and destruction left by a disaster, such as war or disease.
2. Sallie Holmes went back to the United States because she was depressed about not knowing whether her son was dead or alive.

3. Lottie made friends with the people in P'ingtu by baking sugar cookies for them.

Chapter Eleven

1. Recuperate means to recover or get better.
2. Lottie made up the slogan "Thirty Seed-sowers for North China."
3. Southern Baptist women and a group of influential pastors helped establish the Woman's Missionary Union.

Chapter Twelve

1. Inexplicably means in a manner that is impossible to explain.
2. Lottie went to Sha-ling to protect Dan Ho-Bang from his angry relatives.
3. The Christians in Sha-ling were stunned when Li Show-ting became a Christian because Li Show-ting had been a Confucianist scholar who had set out to convince his uncle that Christian beliefs were foolish.

Chapter Thirteen

1. Exuberant means full of joy or happiness.
2. The group Tarleton Crawford formed was called the Gospel Mission.
3. Lottie waited six months before speaking so that she could rest. She feared that if she did not rest she would never be strong enough to return to China.

Chapter Fourteen

1. Quaint means having an old-fashioned charm.

2. The First Baptist Church of Macon, Georgia, provided most of the money for the hospital.
3. Lottie refused to retire in the United States because she believed China was her real home.

Chapter Fifteen

1. Antagonism is a hostility or opposition to something or someone.
2. Red is the color of celebration in China.
3. The Foreign Mission Board was constantly short of money because it relied on pledges that pastors and churches were unable to fulfill.

Chapter Sixteen

1. Hallucinations are experiences of seeing or hearing something that does not really exist.
2. The Manchu Dynasty ruled China for 267 years.
3. Lottie was horrified at what the Christians were doing because she believed all religious persecution was wrong.

Chapter Seventeen

1. Evoking means calling to mind or suggesting an image of something.
2. The annual Christmas Offering was renamed in honor of Lottie Moon in 1918.
3. After Lottie's death, Southern Baptists tried to make amends by erecting stone and glass tributes to her.